I Hate Myself: Self Love is Literal

By Brittany C. Briggs

Preface:

I would say that my parents never gave me clear lines of discipline. I would hear it from my mom if I didn't clean something properly. I would hear it from my dad if I was being annoying when he was tired. But I would rarely hear "Brittany if you do this, this will be the consequence". Besides this one time when my dad picked me up from school, in the seventh grade, he talked about maintaining a good reputation as a woman and how some guys would tell me that they loved me but the truth is that real love is much more rewarding. Furthermore, when young people do not get this clear communication they may allow their mind to believe that the mistakes that come in life were destined and not simply because of lack of discipline. The consequences of life can be categorized as karma. We all experience consequences but different religious outlets might describe this as karma or "the devil". I can honestly say that the reason that I started to hate myself was because of my personal disconnect with consequences. We can all say that the programming of society will allow us to believe certain aspects. We believe that drugs are "bad" unless the doctor prescribes it but the recent opioid crisis will acknowledge this as a myth. We believe that we need others to love us to be worthy. We even believe that teen pregnancy is a bad thing when the generations before us were married by 14. Society programming is something that we all need to decipher through when we are trying to access our true self. But we have to consider the internet and the role its playing on our psyche with this society programming. Social media is dictating our lives and we are embracing this communication era with influenced information without questioning the credibility. We use this information in our every day lives and never evaluate our lifestyles until we see the "toxicity". This impact of the toxicity makes us become present in our experience and feel something about the circumstance. I say the hate appears then. We see the way we hate ourselves when we notice the toxicity that we have embraced because this toxic behavior provided the toxicity. The behavior is a result of the human in you. You caused the toxicity in your life despite not saying "I want this toxicity in my life" you are being care less when you do not use discernment in the decisions that you make for your life. When you can care less bout your "life" the decisions that you make for "your" life then you can see the self hate. "Wow I hate myself because I do not love myself enough to use discernment in this situation to choose something that will not be toxic for me." We can see this when we pour tons of alcohol in our stomachs on weekends knowing that alcohol is full of toxic additives but our desire is to "feel good" for the moment. When that night is over we can probably recollect the activities of our drunk behavior and 9/10 times identify some toxicity in the behavior even if its as minimal as not remembering the awesome sex that your boyfriend say that you all had. Or let's take it a step closer, the way we ruin our daily experiences by chasing money. Many of us choose jobs to help us with our finances. We spend all damn day at these jobs just to realize that its causing us stress, making us anxious, and leading us down a path of destructive depression. This destructive behavior does not result in love! And when you don't love yourself who else will? So how did I find my self love. Or how do I continue to curate my self love? I identify the experiences that I am presently in and analyze everything about it during the process. So for instance I meet a guy that says he wants to take me out. I converse with the man and on our first conversation he explains that he is currently dealing with the mother of his child and their issues. I should then do some discernment. If I say no to this date am I acting out of fear of being the next baby momma or am I showing self love by not participating in the fuck boy activities? There 's no right or wrong answer just merely the best interest of your heart. If it turn down this one date and get two more dates in line simply because I chose myself instead of being distracted by the drama. The fuck boy could have swept me off my feet and had me in the house watching his baby, fighting the baby momma and losing out on experiences that I could have curated for myself. And let's be honest when you get involved in a relationship where there was some toxicity before you arrived you then try to "fix" the problem. This is not your damn problem to fix. Now some may say that that is not love. But others will say I chose to love myself! The same way the people in the toxic situation should have chosen to love themselves. Afterall, if you do not love yourself no one can love you! It is not my assignment to do what the divine does for us. I can not control the toxicity of someone else but I can control the toxicity that I bring to the table.

This book is for my students, my younger self, my older self, my cousins and any woman or man that can relate.

Also, the life of black individuals in America has always mattered. But today we must remind others. We must remind every human being that to hate me is to hate yourself because I am love.

Emotional Abuse:

I love you

But I'm not in love with you

I want to make love to you

But I'm not in love with you

I want you to love me

But I'm not in love with you

I want you to support me

But I'm not in love with you

I want you to answer every call and text

But I'm not in love with you

I want you to give me your body on command

But I'm not in love with you

I hate you

I hate myself

What's love?

Well you know…Emotional Abuse

I think emotional abuse is subjective. However, for me you know its basically when someone makes it seem like they care about my well being but truly just want something from me. No matter if that want is sex, money, time or whatever it is just that they do not love me for real because love is more than a want from someone you know what I mean? Love is like everything other than that want. Love is the way you respond to me. The way you protect me from certain things rather it be danger or rain. Love is the way you look at me in the morning when I'm natural. Love is the way that you make sure I'm comfortable. Love can be when you ask me 'have you eaten?' Because you genuinely want to make sure I feel good and well. I think we lose sight of real love because of the way society tells us we should be loved. For men to show their love to women they must pay x amount of dollars for their dates and buy very expensive gifts. For women to show their love for men they must take on a lot of things including cheating, distance and immaturity.

Although, I'm not totally against men buying expensive gifts. I actually love expensive things. If a man doesn't buy it for me I will buy it for myself. However, I think self love is something that I need more in a relationship than anything else. I cannot put my expectations on a man anymore. It is one of those lessons that I needed to learn the hard way. You have to be able to identify what you need from people to form a relationship that works for you. When you actually sit down and write down your needs or things that you can live without in your marriage or commitment then you can finally see where you are going with your partnerships. This can be useful for any type of relationship. Even if it is a familial situation. For instance, you must know what you will or will not take from your mom that is not the best communicator. So in this sense we have to decide what is best for our individual perspective. In the USA we have free will as humans. The free will should be expressed or experienced or people will begin to resent one another. Within this free will we should have our personal guidelines to follow in order to be happy with our own thought process.

For instance, if I actually like the fact that my husband speaks with other women on the phone because I am usually busy and would rather not hear about his day, then I would not think it was cheating for my husband to speak with multiple women on the phone. We have to decide what is important to us and communicate that. Now something that I realized didn't bother me as much as society told me it should is the amount of money a man spends on me. It's truly something that I can care less about because I feel like it is sort of gold digging. Although, most guys don't have gold to dig, it's interesting to expect a man to pay $250 for a date when he has bills to pay with a regular income.

Perhaps checking up on our own abusive habits is the key here. If we all set our boundaries to fit our best interest and communicated those boundaries, then maybe we will all have a respect for one another wishes. Also, with this upfront thinking we can also identify like minded thinking and gravitate towards people that may want the same things as we do. The cause of your emotional abuse is you and ultimately you are the person with the lasting effect.

Emotional Abuse:

- Makes you feel like you're not good enough

- Constantly threatens to leave you unless you do what they say

- Threatens to hurt you, themselves or others if you leave. (Reach Out)

According to researchers at verywellmind, "When emotional abuse is severe and ongoing, a victim may lose their entire sense of self, sometimes without a single mark or bruise. Instead, the wounds are invisible to others, hidden in the self-doubt, worthlessness, and self-loathing the victim feels. In fact, research indicates that the consequences of emotional abuse are just as severe as those from physical abuse" (Gordon). I disagree with the fact that the wounds are invisible to others. We see this often when we look at our friends or family members that are in tumultuous relationships. On the outside looking in we can see that our loved one is selling themselves short by being mistreated. We can see their once lively personality fade into someone that we no longer recognize. One of the more evident things is that we all have been victim to emotional abuse. Think back to the time you let someone in your life misuse you emotionally.

Who in your life are you allowing to deplete you
emotionally?

_____

_____

_____

_____

_____

_____

_____

_____

_____

_____

_____

_____

I Hate Myself:

Trying to please you:

I lost everything I worked for

Now what do I do

Pick up the bags that I filled

Knowing that you weren't real

I hate myself:

Fighting for fake love

Thinking you were sent from above

I hate myself!

Look at me?

This way I never felt

And when it comes to chance

I won't try again

Because In the rain I dance

Like James Baldwin

Sonny's blues I see the light

I no longer fight-

For love

I am love-

d like no other

Valued by my mother

Father too! Let's go

Get out of this boat

The water is too deep

I'll drown. It only touches my feet

Get away from the illusion

Disregard the delusion

I'm alive.

Ya Know Sometimes Its You

I think it is easy to fall into the realm of self hate when we are following the constraints of society. When we are not thinking for ourselves and operating in our own greatest good. I think its naïve to believe that life is designed for us already and when we wake up everyday the blueprint is laid out for us. I do think we should spend more time cultivating the lifestyle that we want. When we decide to look at others for our well being we start to resent people. Sometimes within that resentment we forget to point our fingers at the one that spewing the hate speech. I know I've been victim to the "I hate you". "You make my life miserable." "I can't believe you did this to me." And then sulking in this rhetoric without realizing these words that I am using are not solutions just attacks. Whenever you attack someone in your humanity you are attacking yourself. What you do to others you are naturally doing to yourself. Calling someone a moron is basically calling yourself a moron because you are dealing with this known moron. Would a smart person pursue a relationship with a moron? We have to be honest with our hate and figure out the direction in which it is truly is going.

I say self hate is a big thing that human being deals with. Self hate is when you constantly put yourself through painful situations knowing that you don't like the feeling. It's like you are telling yourself that you're not good enough for a change.

In order to set the tone for the emotional support that you want you have to set boundaries. The only way that you are going to reach the boundaries that will be most effective is if you know what you need from someone emotionally. Once you actually solidify your wants and needs emotionally then you can move forward to setting boundaries. Now when you are unsure about what it is that you need emotionally there's no humanly possibly way that someone will be able to identify what you actually need or don't need emotionally. However, we do run into those people where we communicate our boundaries and they still tend to push those limits. I consider those people bad for business and we should cease all communication with those type of individuals.

What do you usually do when people overstep and enter your forsaken space? Do you open your hands up wide to see if this person means you any good? "For heaven's sake God brought them into my life, they must be here for a reason." Sometimes this thinking is problematic because what about the test? What about the times where we are being tested? Times that we are at the edge of breaking through and the guilty pleasure strolls through with the most intriguing appearance? Those are the times that are most important in my book. When you reach the point of no return with your boundaries. That point where no one can move them, not even your mother. Then you are at a peace and whole. You know your strength and you

know that you can love again.

Suicide & Women:

Are we all aware that "over the past decade, suicide has been ranked as the 10th leading cause of death in the U.S. across all ages. However, in 2016 it became the second leading cause of death among individuals 10 to 34 years of age" (Monaco). The fact that the suicide rate is steady increasing is definitely something for us to think about as we maneuver through our lives perpetuating a victimhood that could be caused by us.

When I first started this project I wanted to talk about being single at 30 years old. One of the main reasons was because of society constraints. At my age, although I feel pretty young, people seem to judge me for the lifestyle I have chosen to live. Personally, having kids and being married right now would be detrimental to my mental space. There's so much that I'm striving for that to complicate that with others that may depend on me is crippling to my goals. However, I understand the pressure that women are facing as they go through life attempting to meet their personal and professional needs.

The rate of suicide rate is increasing and "Although this increase was seen in both sexes, women had a notably steeper rise in suicide rate during this time -- a 50% increase from 2000 to 2016, and increases were seen across all age groups. For the first several years, women saw an average 2% annual increase in suicide rate, which then jumped to a 3% annual rise from 2007 on" (Monaco).

I can't help but to think that we've allowed our lack of self love to take us to these points. When we don't put pressure on ourselves to love us first and to make sure we handle what needs to be taken care of so that we can be whole, we will continue to kill ourselves. It's no way to live if you are not living for yourself. Many people are dying because they're scared to live. We truly only get one life in this lifetime. No need to live in such disdain of yourself that you want to kill it.

To 30 somethings all around the world. Your life is meaningful without a romantic relationship and a baby. You were already whole when you were born. Don't kill yourself trying to reach a particular goal that may not be the route your life path is going.

Values:

What do you value?

I value myself?

I value my life?

I don't value?

There's been a mistake in my value system. I forgot what it was that I was supposed to pay attention to.

Pay attention to.

Pay attention to myself.

Pay attention to my wants!

I forgot about everything!

Because love is cool

But love ain't it.

Well You Know…Values

When we consider loving ourselves we have to own the fact that sometimes we forget about us as we love other people. Its kind of funny when we consider the things that we value in relationships. We value other people and their happiness. You know when you are sitting back waiting for someone to acknowledge how happy you make them? When we are waiting to hear the I love you because we want to make sure we are valued by the other person in the relationship, when we rarely consider our own feelings until they are hurt? One of the biggest things that we have to remember in a relationship is that we must protect ourselves. When we are protecting ourselves we our loving ourselves instead of just valuing love. We usually value love right? We usually make sure that the person that we want to love us are satisfied if we find value in them. However, we forget to put ourselves first. Even in those painful days when the person that we are in relations with

is not showing up for us in the way that we need them to
we must value ourselves instead of them. I think this is
something that young women like myself lose sight of
when we get involved in romantic relationships. We even
lose sight of this with relationships that people tell us we
should value.

This falls in the realm of relationships with our
parents. Sometimes we have the volatile relationships with
our parents that we know are not in our best interest and we
do not effectively communicate these issues because we do
not want to interrupt these relationships or impact them
negatively. Sometimes it takes for us to value ourselves a
bit more than the relationship in order to present our best
selves. Have you ever been involved in a relationship that
was so toxic that it caused terrible anxiety? You focused
more on the person or the situation at hand i.e cheating,
financial needs. When we focus more on the person or
issues within our relationship than our own well being we

are distracted and by default not focusing on the greater good for ourselves. These feelings or perspectives can cause us to lose sight on the things in our lives that help us mobilize.

The poem 'I Hate Myself' really focuses on the impacts of not focusing on yourself in a relationship. In this poem there's a lot of the blame game here. The truth of the matter is self hate is a result of your own perspective of yourself. Its time to take responsibility and the power back from the scenarios. Yes, it is clear that when you chase after someone who repeatedly tell you that they do not want to be in a relationship, or constantly do things that go against your relationship values, it is ultimately your choice. We make these choices that leave us feeling like less of a person instead of making choices to remove certain individuals from our lives or distancing from certain relationships with these individuals as a fulfillment for the things that we value which can be the relationship and not necessarily ourselves.

Some times we don't even value the individual we value the idea of them. For instance, in a romantic relationship where the partner does not demonstrate the same values as you and in fact takes pride in not demonstrating these values you may make excuses for this individual. Some excuses can be "well they grew up differently", "They still need to learn". But the fact of the matter is that they do not value the same things that you do when it comes to a relationship so either you need to compromise or slide out of this relationship because you will be unhappy. Making excuses can look like you value the relationship more than yourself. When you are not thinking about your greater good then you are not expressing self love, you're expressing self hate for yourself. This tends to boil over in your relationship where you start to blame the partner simply because they have different values.

Again, this is where boundaries come into play. There is a big need for boundaries to be set within your own perspective. Get rid of what your mom wants for you, your dad wants for you or what your boyfriend wants for you, consider what you want for yourself. How do I feel loved? How do people show me love? How can I express love? How do I like for people to express love to me?

Now having a mentality that only considers our individual self can be considered selfish right? But remember if we are all being selfish with our perspectives as we head towards the greater good would that not that result in the greater good for everyone? I think when we focus on the other person we are not able to see our boundaries clearly. What constraints can we put in place to make sure only our values are being met? When do we decide to compromise? This can also be placed within the boundaries.

Values and Summer Walker

Every time, I think about Value I think about Summer Walker's 'I will kill you' song. I particularly think the song is amazing but the lyrics are really problematic. Recently someone that I know was arrested and is on trial for allegedly helping her boyfriend kill her roommate. So I start to think about values. What are we valuing when we start to perpetuate certain behaviors that lead us to "hell and jail" about a boy? Walker implies that she had never had a love like the one that the boy was displaying to her. However, from the lyrical content it doesn't seem like that was love at all. When we value ourselves would we "go to hell and back for you, Bend over backwards, acrobats for you" (Mamo)? I honestly don't think that we will do those things for men that are not doing the same for us if we truly value ourselves. Actually I don't think we would do that for anyone if we actually valued ourselves. Just imagine your best friend making it difficult for you two to hangout.

Wouldn't you no longer have a best friend.

Can't sleep:

I drug myself to bed

Praying for a better day

Hoping to here you say

I love you but i tread

Lightly through my social

The others say

They are being hopeful

For the day

The day that the dead

Awakes and sees the truth

That it was me that loved you

Well you know...can't sleep

I think its time for us to talk about our dark periods you know? Like the times when we are dealing with some things and we just want to be in a negative space about it. I don't think those are times that we are out of character. In fact, to me it is the complete opposite; the times where we show people what else we are capable of when are safety is threatened. I think people and situations can bring our dark sides out and within that darkness we need to be able to navigate. For example, say you gave a guy your everything and he ends up gaslighting you like you're some average woman. ("Gaslighting is a tactic in which a person or entity, in order to gain more power, makes a victim question their reality" (Sarkis Ph.D.))

You're not an average woman and with that you respond negatively. You yell at him and scream and get defensive. You start calling him names that you definitely shouldn't, but you don't feel bad for doing so, even after you've completely made a fool of yourself. Come on sis you don't have to feel bad when someone has wronged you. I think the problem is that you were out of control. The behavior you displayed was not the behavior that you're proudest of as you reflect on how far you've come in life. I also think the issue here is the accountability. If you don't own the fact that you didn't necessarily love the way you behaved, then you will not be able to adjust in future events. The truth is we should control ourselves because it is an example of self love. Discipline is self love. Being able to trust ourselves to be the people that we want to be is self love. We shouldn't harp on ourselves for reacting in the way that we want to and not feeling sorry for it. We should be mindful of our actions and be willing to grow from them. The dark times build character.

I think we only feel bad for our dark moments for the way that we presented ourselves. That could be shallow. Do we have to be these fictional people that society asks us to be? No and especially not in the states. We live in a free country where we do exactly what we want to do. Just think about all of the Americans that just seem like wearing a mask is infringing on their "free" rights. This attitude is embedded in our culture and we should use it on more than mask. We should use it when we feel confined and/ or in fear that someone will judge us. However, those consequences can be painful.

I think when you get to the point where there are serious consequences for your actions then there's definitely a cycle of self hate taking place and no longer just learning curves. The Saturn return is something that I have been dealing with and it has really highlighted my self hate issues. "The Saturn Return is when the planet Saturn comes back to meet your natal Saturn. It takes about 29.5 years for this slow-mover to return to where it was when you were born. The Saturn return hits in the late 20s and its impact is felt into the early 30s (Hall)"

It's really helping me identify with a lot of my flaws and lovely attributes. A flaw that I have recognized is that I usually allow people to be emotionally controlling in my life because I can see them for who they are. It's the beauty of being a humanities major, I can see people even when they can't see themselves and I love to do it which is the problematic aspect. I have definitely been the girl waiting for the guy to see what he has been missing. Wanting him to realize that I was the prize and that everything around him was just a figment of his imagination. However, these guys never see what they have been missing because they are setting their boundaries for what works for them. The truth is we are not every one's cup of tea. You can be the best thing smoking and still not be someone's choice and its hateful to yourself to sit around and wait for a man to see you for who you are when you should be busy being the best version of yourself.

You know when we focus on ourselves we pull ourselves out of the dark places earlier. Sometimes we don't even reach the dark spaces because they are not relevant in our experiences. For example, the guy that gas lighted you wouldn't have been able to gas light you in the first place. That guy told you and showed you who he was many times before. You decided to see the best in him and hope that he saw the best in you. If you would have walked away immediately when you noticed, he didn't have your best interest at heart then you wouldn't be in the current position. Let's do better for us sis! Can't fall victim to the games if we don't play along.

This is when we mention boundaries again right. We have to really set boundaries and be disciplined with these boundaries to establish our self love. The fact of the matter is that self love is truly literal. We have to cultivate the experience that we want. What is self love to you. Self love to me is loving everything about me. The good, the bad, and the ugly. Loving myself and the way I look naturally. Loving myself enough to be hygienic and moisturize my skin. Loving myself enough to create a daily ritual that benefits me while helping me manifest all of my desires. Self love is the positive days and the negative days as long as I see myself in this experience. Self love is the pain that I endure for loving myself and being rejected by those that are hateful to themselves. We have to figure out what is our version of love you know? So tell me what do you love about your self?

Gen Z and Mental Health

The Gen Z's are some of my most favorite people. I love their attitude when it comes to being direct and overt. Most people will probably disagree as they are some of the most relentless people alive today. They are singlehandedly changing the world that we once knew for the better by demanding racism end. However, after being a professor for a few years it's apparent that Gen Z's are extremely at risk of mental health declines if they aren't already suffering. During my most recent semester teaching over 6 of my 65 students went out on medical leaves after being checked into psychiatric hospitals. And stats similar to the following from psychology.com tell us why.

According to Psychology.com, students are not getting enough sleep and "one 2014 study analyzed approximately 28,000 8th, 10th, and 12th graders from Fairfax County, Virginia. In their study, students reported on average 6.5 hours of sleep per school night, with only 3 percent reporting that they received the recommended 9 hours per night. Moreover, a 2016 review found that teens gradually lose sleep every year. Specifically, the study indicated that teens lost about 90 minutes of sleep each school night from about ages of 11-12 to about 17-18" (Horan).

Gen Z's have to start taking care of their bodies better. As we know "simply put, Gen Z has been accruing astronomical amounts of sleep debt for years. Sleep debt, otherwise known as sleep loss, occurs when an individual fails to attain the recommended number of hours of sleep for his or her age" (Horan). Sleep debt is something that people laugh at because it doesn't make sense to people that are not progressive thinkers. There have been misconceptions that if you don't sleep that you have a better chance at greatness. We know that these are just not the facts. Sleep debt is a quite simple concept when broken down. "For example, the recommended minimum number of hours of sleep for adolescents is 9. If a teen were only to sleep five hours per night Monday through Friday, by Saturday, he or she would already be in 20 hours of sleep "debt" (Horan).

Over It:

Ya know it's comes a time

When you're drinking wine

Thinking that it was love

It's was nothing like love

This smile on my face

Thinking of tomorrow and today

My future is bright

The future is tight

Cuz my money getting long

Opportunities arising

And though I'm all alone

Loving me is easy er then dying

I was dying but now I'm free

Out here just living as me

You Ever Just Been Over It? Like I'm done...gots ta go!

Moving on is one of those crazy experiences that really require us to be disciplined. But before we can even move on we have to come to the understanding that what we had is not what we need. I think the hardest part is realizing that the person that you love or the idea of the person that you love is the person that is bringing the worst out of you. This individual or family member is someone that triggers all of the dark places in you and rarely supports you when you are in your light. The self love that this requires is impeccable because you have to get rid of something that you want because it isn't serving your better good. Think about this like alcohol. In college I knew that alcohol was something that I didn't need but I wanted it often because of the social experience that came with it. However, it came to a point when I graduated that I realized in order to be the best version of myself I had to drop the habit of drinking alcohol with my friends on the weekends because it brought the dark side out of me. Drinking was something that I wanted but something I definitely didn't need to drink. After giving up my habit of drinking I was able to see the clearly. I was able to realize that some of my friends were only around because they liked the dark side. They liked to see me at my worst. I realized that the alcohol was more of an experience that other people thought I needed to be myself. It was brought to my attention that sometimes the people that we surround ourselves with, those that we love are not always the people that we need. So when you get to this point where you get addicted to someone and the experience that you are having with them be mindful of the control this experience has over you. You want to enjoy life and not feed into the drugs. Think about the brighter days despite the loss of the wants. When you finally get rid of the people in your life that should not be there things start to fall into place. I remember getting rid of exes and getting job offers shortly

after. The universe is here to meet us where we are.

Don't Kill Him Sis

He's trying to take you there.
Trying to see the depths that you will go.
Sis Don't Kill Him
He's trying to turn you into a monster.
Trying to make you into an animal.
Sis Don't Kill Him
He's trying to be a man
Trying to find his manhood through your pain
Sis Don't Kill Him
He's trying to get a head
Trying to find his bread in your cabinetry
Sis Don't Kill Him
Don't kill yourself neither
Don't let this world make you violent sis!
Be the gem and leave the rock alone!
Society will tell you what you want
Society will tell you what they don't
Society will let you die
Society will let you lie
Society won't save you
Society won't bathe you
Because life is yours to live
Because life is yours to give
Because life is yours
Appreciate this life
Appreciate this time
Don't lose it in the future
Stay here! Grow here! Don't die in the future.

That Deadly Love

You ever killed yourself for some love? I think that's the most dramatic stuff ever. Society keeps telling women that they are less than if they are not married by a certain time. We suffer for love and in the end we have nothing to show for it because we weren't being ourselves. I think authenticity is a big thing that we lack today and within this lack we find ourselves lost. Lost souls seem to be the most hateful don't they? Do you agree that when we are not truly being ourselves and/or following our needs we get lost and because we are lost we start reacting? The reaction is us trying to find something outside of ourselves that makes us comfortable being someone else. We will never find that thing. Authenticity will be our true sense of freedom, until then we will seek happiness that is pretty unattainable.

Have you ever had a middle age coworker that you felt had it all together? They had the nice house, long term marriage and beautiful kids but they were extremely unhappy. I start to think that those women didn't take the time out to figure out what they wanted out of life before they decided to fall victim to society's pressures. I think it's important to make sure that we are happy with the choices that we make. Ideas are important to have and we should have our own. If we never figure out what we want we will start to resent ourselves and our life.

I think we have to set boundaries on the society pressures we listen to. We should set boundaries on the people that we trust to communicate effective information to us. Its time to take responsibility for our actions.

Women & The Game of Life

The biggest stumbling blocks for women after a painful break-up are:

- not really wanting to move on.

- not knowing how to move on.

If you have just gotten out of a relationship and are going through a break up its about time that you consider a plan to get you through this mess. You don't want to double back. You don't want to make the same mistake over again because we know it's just going to end the same way it did the last time (Orloff).

According to Dr. Orloff you should "…accept that it's over and focus your energy on creating a positive new life for yourself without your ex" (Orloff).

Following these 10 steps may help you move on and get on with the rest of your life:

1. Accept it

Sis, let it go. I know that's easier said than done. Put on your best outfit. Do your hair up nice, flick it up and post them on your social media site. Get you a little attention to remember who you are. But accept that this break up is real and know that you will love again.

2. Distance yourself

Delete him from social media. Block him from your phone. Maybe in a few years you won't mind seeing him on your newsfeed but for now he doesn't need access to you because you are healing.

3. Stop talking about him

Fuck him! Like every time he pops up in your head just self talk "fuck him" because even if he's a great guy he isn't great for you.

4. Skip the blame game

At the end of the day it's your fault sis. You chose him.

Even if he cheated you still chose the clown. No need to

blame anyone.

5. Learn from it

Make sure that you don't date the same guy twice.

Learning from a bad dating experience is really what dating

is about. Don't feel bad because it didn't workout but do

embrace the lessons you learned.

6. Picture yourself over him

Imagine what it would be like if you were completely over

him. How would you be acting? Where would you live?

What would you eat? What would you wear? Think about

the greatness your freedom has bestowed upon you. You

will be just fine.

7. Focus on yourself

Remember that hobby that you loved? What about the passion project that you thought you didn't have enough time for last summer? You don't have any distractions (besides your job) so get to it. Maybe you will win an award that lands you in the city's newspaper and your ex will have to deal with seeing you on the news at 10 am, 5pm , 7pm and 10pm for a week straight.

8. Get out there!

Even during the pandemic people are dating so if you are reading this during COVID-19 use social media. If you are reading this post COVID-19 take yourself out every weekend this month. Sit at the bar all dolled up. Talk to those that seem interesting.

9. Take it nice and slow

If you don't feel like going out then take a night off. There is no rush to replace your ex. You just want to be whole again. So if working on your healing (not sulking in pity) is what you need to do please do that.

10. Don't generalize and don't compare

No need to make this a one size fits all situation and don't go into every situation thinking that they all are going to be the same. To really get to know people you can't compare you have to take the time out to see them in their light (Orloff).

On Being Brought from Pontiac to Auburn Hills:

Never thought I'd agree with Wheatley

Wait I don't

But I remember getting baptized

Two years after I arrived

I felt alive

I felt reenergized

But the Bible didn't save me

I saved myself with belief

Belief that I was she

That I was her

That I wasn't the person

That they told me I was

That they told me I had to be

Like do what all black girls does

Ratchet girl

Nappy girl

Ignorant girl

Fat girl

They love the Bible too

It's hard for me to do

What those hateful people do

I remember I was baptized

My life was a surprise

I was a part of group

I belonged too

Never have I belonged

Always the weird girl

Always the loud girl

Always the wild girl

I remember that girl

She was so lost

Now she's home

Happy to be here

Crying tears of joy

Do You Truly Believe?

We put a lot of our beliefs into belief systems or religions. I see nothing wrong with that. However, I do think it shows your lack of self love when you think you don't deserve something because of that belief system. For instance, if you grew up Muslim and feel that your blessings are not coming fast enough because you have chosen to drink alcohol despite your religious confinements. I think that the thought process behind this is a bit hard to understand and possibly detrimental to your self respect. Conditioning yourself to speak negatively to yourself and be emotionally damaging to yourself is difficult to maneuver through. You have to be kind to yourself despite your mishaps or lack of tradition. I see people regularly beat themselves up for not meeting the needs of the religion that their parents pushed on them when they were first born. Please pursue life through the vision that is best for you, not the vision that is best for your parents.

When you are not kind to yourself you start to hate yourself. Let's be honest there are enough individuals out there that just don't like us and they are usually not kind at all. We should not be like those individuals! We must be kind to ourselves and respect ourselves. Speak life into ourselves and use positive affirmations regularly.

I think there should be a pact set within yourself to never let another belief system change the way you feel about yourself. We should utilize these systems to grow as people not to become self haters. If your religion is not making you a better version of yourself then maybe you should reevaluate your choice of beliefs.

Religion

As we know, especially as American citizens that
Christianity plays a pretty large role in our lives. Even if
you claim to not be influenced my Christianity you can
easily take a dollar out of your pocket and read "In God We
Trust". In fact, "Christians remained the largest religious
group in the world in 2015, making up nearly a third (31%)
of Earth's 7.3 billion people, according to a new Pew
Research Center demographic analysis" (Hackett and
McClendon). These are very influential numbers and we
have to consider where has society grown or lack the
growth under these Christian values.

One thing to make note of is "…the number of
Christians in what many consider the religion's heartland,
the continent of Europe, is in decline" (Hackett and
McClendon).

Even more noteworthy, "Globally, Muslims make up the second largest religious group, with 1.8 billion people, or 24% of the world's population, followed by religious "nones" (16%), Hindus (15%) and Buddhists (7%). Adherents of folk religions, Jews and members of other religions make up smaller shares of the world's people" (Hackett and McClendon).

The fact of the matter is that there are many different religions that the human race practice and it would not behoove me or anyone else to be inconsiderate to other human beings. Knowing that other religions exist, its important to compare and contrast some of the belief systems to see how they are similar more than their differences. These similarities is what help the community. The differences can be a sore spot in some communities but all in all are the true pioneers of growth when they are accepted.

Yes You Are a Woman:

You're a woman ms truth

They just were intimidated by you

You were strong

You were wise

You were resilient

And I'm a woman too

Fighting with myself everyday in everyway

Trying to forget the love that wasn't shown

I no longer question my womanly nature

Because he said I was too manly

Because she said I was too ugly

Ima woman because I'm here to stay

I stand my ground on both feet

With my head held high and see

The sun is closer than you think

It's nearly here to protect me

The rays have me higher than them

Those that can't see me see that I'm

A woman ya know one that phenomenal

One that enters the room and commands all

Even on her worse day

She's a beast at life but she's not strong

She's tired of fighting so she sits

And when they tell her to stand

She still sits

Because it's on her time now

It's her world now

You're just a squirrel

The squirrel seeking its pleasure

I don't want to quarrel

Because I'm tirelessly running

Running from the woman that I want to be

Because it was a question above my head for so long

I forgot to feel in the blanks

That empty spot was numb

I'm still writing but it's coming along

Got some work to do but it's getting done

Phenomenal Woman

Maya said some things about being a phenomenal woman. I took those things with me. You know being phenomenal can be in your own right. I think we all go through those times when we feel like we are the shit! Like can't nobody tell us nothing. We get dressed up for the party and know that we are going to shut it down.

What about the times that you get ready for the office? You know that you are going to be the flyest one there so it is nothing for you to get up and get out of the house in enough time to grab donuts for the office. Those are the times that its easiest to love ourselves. But we should also love ourselves on those days where the outer appearance just isn't doing it for us. On those days when we want to stay home and lounge around in our sweats. Why on our less productive days do we conduct negative self talk? We call ourselves lazy and describe our experiences as one where we are not fulfilling our necessities? For instance, at, this very moment I'm beating myself up by stressing my mind and body because it's a Sunday and I need to respond to some emails that I have been neglecting this past week. Sometimes we just have to be kind to ourselves.

Leave it for everyone else to be our enemies. We don't need to be our own enemies right? I think when we can't see our greatness on a regular basis that we just aren't seeing ourselves. What's the block? Where is the misconception? Is the media leading us to believe that we are not enough for ourselves? I think sometimes this can be the case. Especially when you're a single woman and the television basically tells you that you must not be of quality because you don't have a man. Or when you're in a position of bettering yourself but you aren't fully developed. You are still in areas struggling and your work isn't currently fruitful. People will bring you down and society won't be too far away with their media production resembling common thoughts of people and their likings. The media is nothing but a regurgitation of the masses beliefs and it leaves little to no room for the out of the box thinkers.

This is the time where we disregard others. If we are strong enough to give ourselves the love that we want from other people, then maybe we will be able contribute that same love to others. Until then, we must be able to use discernment and to disregard the information that people provide that's not particularly helpful for us. I know too many times where I gave up on my thoughts because someone told me they were dumb. Don't listen to other people, use their suggestions if you are sure that they have your best interest at heart but do not let them make permanent decisions for your life. Follow your mind and make things happen that represent you. Stop worrying about the masses and tap into your individual happiness and carry it around with you as you integrate into groups.

Never forget yourself and the love that you have for you!

"You know it really doesn't matter how people respond to our pain. I think we give people too much power. A lot of times people are dealing with their own things and they don't have the power or will to deal with our emotions or "problems". I say it's best to focus on what you need and want to be happy. As long as you have the things in your life that make you happy then you can start to give that over pour to others. But don't deplete yourself trying to make people in your life happy. If someone wants to be apart of your life they will adapt to what you bring to the table."

- Brittany

Wrongdoing:

You said you never done me wrong

What about that time you gave me a sad song

You know the time you wanted to be my man

Had me cut off my hoes for you to tell me you was just

playing

I was never faithful to you

You thought I was going to be your fool?

That day you lost me

That night I lost me

I remember you told me that you cared

I remember you told me that we were building

I remember you told me that it was fair

I remember you told me you were healing

Your Wrongdoing or My Wrongdoing

I think we know what we want from people. Although, we know what we want from people we still settle for the bullshit that some people present. But why? Are we doing this because people have told us that we should not want the things that we do? I don't really know why we do it but I feel like it is because we are living in the future and not the present. Every time I think back to a relationship that didn't benefit me and I decided to stay, it was because I was scared of the future. You know scared to be alone. I have always heard about the stories of black women not meeting a mate to marry. So the rejection hits a bit harder each time you are not the chosen one. Although, I have to admit that I'm usually the one leaving the relationship and feeling mistreated if he doesn't chase after me to prove his love that is pretty non-existent.

Not "getting picked" is a crazy way to think about being rejected by some one. How and why would anybody in their right mind give a flawed human being that much power? Sometimes I look back at the craziness that I settled for just to realize that I would have never actually succeeded in these situations but I wanted to be "picked". Putting yourself in this type of competition just shows that you don't value yourself and what it is that you come with. It's time to reclaim who you are and move past the nonsense. Yes, the propaganda on the TV tells us that we are not valuable without the ideal man but let's be honest most people that we know with a man is not in an ideal situation.

Not allowing people that type of control just gives us the opportunity to focus on the needs that we have. Sometimes we think that we need people in our lives but we really don't because they haven't added any value. These people may be leeches that are sucking you dry, but you are addicted to the pain that comes with the motion. Being addicted to pain is a whole other can of worms. What we have to do is to keep them boundaries in place. After all ladies we want to be satisfied and not content. Forget about the relationship if there is no equity. I know for myself that the relationship would never workout anyways. After I got what I wanted from the dude such as a commitment I'd come up with all types of reasons why he's the problem. The truth is we know who our people are and we are too busy trying to impress people that don't matter by not being honest with ourselves and others.

The Humanitarian

A humanitarian is someone "having concern for or helping to improve the welfare and happiness of people" (Dictionary.com). If the person is not a humanitarian, I don't know if I can trust them to have my best interest at heart on most occasions. Sometimes we have to consider the motivation of people. One of the most noticeable things when researching about humanitarians is that there a many different definitions to live by. It's apparent that humanitarians can even be confused on their purpose. While taking a look at corp members responses to "what is a humanitarian to you?" One of the responses included, "For me being a humanitarian means to have human values and an understanding of all human situations that we share, regardless of race, ethnicity, religion and social status. It's working towards common human goals and ensuring we support people with respect and dignity" (Mercy Corps). One of the other corps members suggested that "A humanitarian is able to identify people's needs and vulnerability with empathy for them. They're passionate about walking the extra mile to help alleviate the suffering of those in the midst of a crisis" (Mercy Corps).

If a person is not putting my well being in perspective, I can't trust them with my life. No matter if you are my friend or my man, I need you to be a humanitarian for my life. We must hold people to a higher standard. After all, Frederick Douglas' wife gave us the blueprint when she wouldn't marry a slave. She helped Douglas escape slavery and go into hiding in free states so they could be married. It is time for women to demand that men break free from the chains of patriarchy and misogyny and to embrace real love so that we can grow fruitful families instead of pools of toxic mess.

Despite the pain:

Ya know I love you right

Still only want your love

Funny how life turned us into enemies

I thought time was plenty

But we too stubborn to assist each other

In life because we have choices

This buffet of noises

Despite The Pain

So is it love if I crave the pain? I always wonder about the love and hate relationship. I don't think I've ever truly hated someone that I loved. I think I hated looking for myself in the love that I couldn't recognize. Sometimes people say that it is Self Hate but really I think it is giving yourself what you want. If you want the trash bag guy that keeps making you the last priority in a way you are showing yourself the love that you want to show it.

Do you remember the people in your life that triggered you to walk away but they have this soft spot in your heart? I don't think that's self hate I think that's unconditional love. I think that's truly how we show that we love someone. The thing is the person that we were loving definitely missed out on a real one. I know every relationship that I have been in rather it is romantic or strictly platonic they've triggered me to leave or to disconnect but there is always something that keeps me connected for empathy. I think you build a tribe and meet people along the way. We can grow apart but still love people. To me love is respect and community. It's easy to respect someone that has hurt you. It's even easier to believe that they are a part of your community as well.

When it comes to unconditional love if we don't put guidelines in place we will soon find ourselves drowning in the sorrows caused by others. Empathy does not go hand in hand with accepting abuse. Empathizing is always showing respect but it doesn't have to be a compromise for happiness. We have to figure out how to love but how to let people be themselves at the same time. No matter what we want from someone that we love, if they aren't willing to give that to us then we have to accept what they are giving or come to the decision to become distant. A compromise isn't always necessary when you are in pain. A compromise is necessary for a relationship to work. When you no longer see the relationship working, stop compromising.

The Saturn Return

I once read that "Our ego loves those feelings of powerlessness, that keep us hidden and small in a corner- and thus, *safe*. No matter how awake we are, spiritual growth proceeds in a spiral, and at times we're dragged down to purge more of our ego, and then soar to the next level of mastery" (Monica).

Is this what you dealt with from the age 27-30? No matter how hard you tried to get ahead life seemed to always drag you back into this unhappy, not good enough state? There is always a healthy time to figure out where your ego is holding you up at. How are you making these bad decisions repeatedly? Or why do these same type of problems keep occurring in my life? Most of us can contribute this experience to the Saturn return, " when the planet **Saturn** comes back to meet your natal Saturn. It takes about 29.5 years for this slow-mover to return to where it was when you were born. The Saturn return hits in the late 20s and its impact is felt into the early 30s" (Hall). This is a crucial time period in our lives as we get back to our purpose and goal. As we are born to the world our purpose is being cultivated and if we continue to allow our lack of boundaries to disrupt our experiences due to the illusion of freedoms present we will miss out on the abundance that is here for us.

Don't look back:

So it's over you left

Don't look back

Where you're going they can't come

You have a lot to offer and they don't

You're genuine and free

They're illusions and foreseen

Fight for your shit back

Keep it close for an attack

They'll be calling soon

Asking for a redo

But you know life gave you lemons

That fool was fighting demons

You have been lonelier

Don't get comfortable to moan, her

Life is important so don't give up on you

Be happy so do what you gotta do

Cut them off

Leave them for dead

Like that did you

Don't Look Back

Is giving second chances so bad? I mean let's be realistic here. Did they know that they were in the wrong when they did the messed up stuff? In all actuality we take them back out of love and out of fear. Crazy part is we can't operate out of love and fear simultaneously, there comes a time to choose which one is going to work best for you in this situation. I think this is where you see the toxicity in relationships. You know when you just can't get enough of someone but you also can't stand to be around them. I have to ask though. Where is the real love in this situation? Who is benefiting from this fake construct? I mean passion is one thing but love? I don't remember love being so painful to stay in a relationship. I recall pain from unforeseen circumstances like cancer or something.

It has to be hate that we are showing when we operate in this way. I guess we have to ask ourselves are we talking about the way we hate our partners or ourselves?

No way should you even want to go back to a relationship where you don't feel valued, respected or loved. There are just some things that you have to have in order. I look at the decisions that I've made in relationships and my biggest mistake was letting people love me less than I loved myself. We set the standards. And even if their mother has never loved them, their fathers, grandparents, whoever, we don't deserve to be mistreated because of it. Let these unhealthy hearted individuals find the love that they need within themselves. Similar to the way we had to find love in ourselves.

Telling people how we want to be loved is pretty dead these days. I'm not telling anyone how to love me. I'm just going to love myself to the point that if they don't get that its not about them but about my personal well being then they are really not for me. Guys that understand your vibe, get what you need out of the relationship. I have too many guy friends that understand what I want. I get that

I shouldn't be thinking about what other guys are doing when I'm trying to build a relationship with another but I'm just saying. It doesn't take rocket science. Don't let people treat you like you are not the prize. When you are at your best everything about you exudes abundance and if people are not bringing that out of you than they need to keep it moving. It is time to take control of your life. Don't let society tell you where you should be as far as relationships and achievements. Cut the relationship off if its not serving your better good.

Five Reasons to Leave a Toxic Relationship:

1. They Never Change

2. If You Let Them Do It Once, It Will Happen Again

3. You're Wasting Valuable Time

4. Trust Is Broken

5. It Gets Old

Love yourself babes! I'm out! To my students I love you!

To my parents you are awesome! To my brother stay black!

To my niece and nephew thanks for the love (Dennis).

References

Dennis, Sierra. "5 Reasons Why Going Back To Toxic

Relationships Is Never Worth It ." 6 November

2014. *Elite Daily.* 23 July 2020.

Dictionary.com. "humanitarian." 1 January 2020.

Dictionary.com. 23 July 2020.

<https://www.dictionary.com/browse/humanitarian

>.

Gordon, Sherri. "What is Emotional Abuse? ." 20 July

2020. *Verywellmind.* 23 July 2020.

<https://www.verywellmind.com/identify-and-

cope-with-emotional-abuse-4156673>.

Hackett, Conrad and David McClendon. "Christians remain

world's largest religious group, but they are

declining in Europe." 5 April 2017. *Pew Research

Center* . 23 July 2020.

Hall, Molly. "The Saturn Return and Its Significance in

    Astrology ." 31 May 2019. *liveaboutdotcom.* 23

    July 2020.

Horan, Kailey. "Gen Z Is in Serious Debt, but This Time

    It's Not Financial ." 21 February 2020. *Pyschology*

    Today . 23 July 2020.

Mamo, Heran. "Here Are the Lyrics to Summer Walker's

    'I'll Kill You,' Feat. Jhené Aiko." 21 October 2019.

    Billboard. 23 July 2020.

    <https://www.billboard.com/articles/news/lyrics/85

    33712/summer-walker-ill-kill-you-lyrics-jhene-

    aiko>.

Mercy Corps. "We asked our staff: What does being a

    humanitarian mean to you? ." 18 August 2015.

    Mercy Corps . 23 July 2020.

    <https://www.mercycorps.org/blog/what-does-

    being-humanitarian-mean>.

Monaco, Kristen. "Suicide Rate in Women Jumps by 50%."

14 June 2018. *Medpagetoday*. 23 July 2020.

Monica. "THE ART OF JOY PUSHING THROUGH

RESISTANCE ." 15 April 2019. *The White Bench* .

23 July 2020. <https://thewhitebench.com/the-art-

of-joy-pushing-through-resistance/>.

Orloff, Judith. "How To Move On: 10 Steps For Closure

After You Break Up ." 15 November 2017.

EVERYDAY HEALTH. 23 July 2020.

<https://www.everydayhealth.com/emotional-

health/how-move-on-10-steps-closure-after-you-

break-up/>.

Reach Out. "What is emotional abuse? ." 1 January 2020.

Reach Out. 23 July 2020.

<https://au.reachout.com/articles/what-is-

emotional-abuse>.

Sarkis Ph.D., Stephanie. "11 Warning Signs of

Gaslighting." 22 January 2017. *Pyschology Today*.

23 July 2020.

<https://www.psychologytoday.com/us/blog/here-

there-and-everywhere/201701/11-warning-signs-

gaslighting>.

CPSIA information can be obtained
at www.ICGtesting.com
Printed in the USA
LVHW111123310121
677937LV00005B/439